The Last Lamb

Susan Christman

WestBow Press books may be ordered through booksellers or by contacting:

WestBow Press
A Division of Thomas Nelson
1663 Liberty Drive
Bloomington, IN 47403
www.westbowpress.com
1-(866) 928-1240

Because of the dynamic nature of the Internet, any web addresses or links contained in this book may have changed since publication and may no longer be valid. The views expressed in this work are solely those of the author and do not necessarily reflect the views of the publisher, and the publisher hereby disclaims any responsibility for them.

Any people depicted in stock imagery provided by Thinkstock are models, and such images are being used for illustrative purposes only.

Certain stock imagery © Thinkstock.

ISBN: 978-1-4497-3893-8 (sc)

Library of Congress Control Number: 2012901987

Printed in the United States of America

WestBow Press rev. date: 02/03/2012

My mother woke me in her own special way,

"Wake up," she whispered, "Passover begins today."

On Passover we celebrate Moses' leading Israel free,

they were told what to take, what to eat, and what to leave.

A spotless lamb's blood was to cover the door post of the home

so the Angel of Death knew which families to leave alone.

(Exodus 12:1-2, Leviticus 23:4-8, Numbers 9:2-5, Numbers 28:16-25)

My absolute favorite day of all,

is Lamb Selection day, when we go to the newborn stall.

We select the "chosen" lamb, perfect and spot free,

then during Passover, this lamb is offered as

a sacrifice for my family and me.

(Exodus 12:3-6, Exodus 12:21-27)

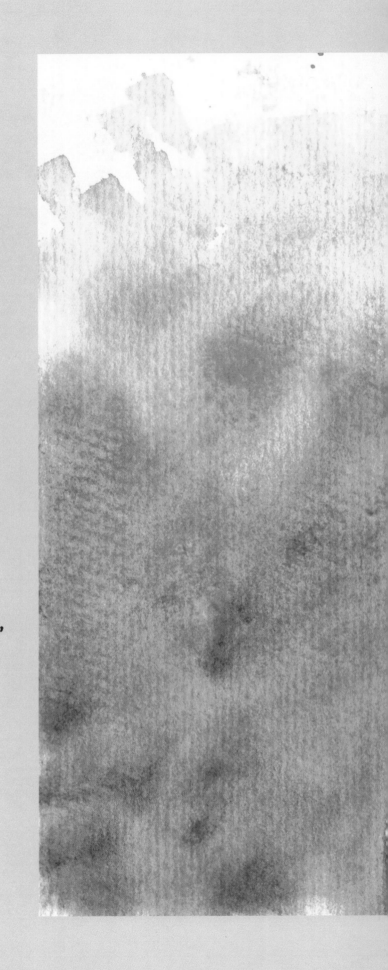

Each year I've asked
and begged to go,

but my Father has always
insisted, "NO!"

However this year, my Father
seems to have changed,

I'm not really sure why, it just
seems kind of strange.

Ever since the new "Rabbi Jesus"
has come into our land,

my Father seems to be a different,
more loving kind of man.

(1 John 4:7)

He said I could go on this
year's Lamb Selection day!

As we left, there were
several people hustling
all in our way.

The city was packed,
such an exciting time,

but I stayed close to
Father, his hand in mine.

(Matthew 20:29,
Matthew 21: 10-11, Mark
10:46, Luke 19:37, John 12:12)

Walking through the city gate, before us we could see,

Rabbi Jesus riding a colt, sitting very majestically.

He entered the city, gentle and mild

as Palm branches were strew before him by a child.

The chant started soft, and then grew louder with each chord,

"Hosanna! Blessed is he who comes in the name of the Lord!"

(Matthew 21:1-11, Mark 11:1-10)

After the loud procession
had passed,

we walked onto the
newborn stall, at last.

There were the lambs,
one-year old males,

running, chasing, and nipping
each other's tails.

My Father said the lamb would
be mine to take care of,

oh, I couldn't wait to pick the
lamb I would tend and love.

If only for a few days, I
would call him my own,

this lamb would be very
important in our home.

This little lamb was special,
but not just to me,

this lamb was chosen as a
sacrifice for my whole family.

(Exodus 12:5)

I choose my perfect lamb; he was as cute as could be,

part of me wanted to just let him run free.

He ran alongside us, tugging at the rope,

kicking up his heels, and baying out all hope.

He finally stopped struggling and snuggled, right by my side.

The rest of the way home, he and I, stride for stride.

The day before Passover
was always spent
cleaning with Mother.

Cleaning the house
of all dirt and leaven,
oh what a bother!

When we had finished,
I fed our perfect lamb
– kissed his head,

closed the pen gate, and
I went straight to bed.

**(Exodus 12:17-20,
Deuteronomy 16:1-4)**

I woke on Passover Day and
went to my tender pet,

knowing today would be my
last with him – and yet?

When I went out to his pen,
he was nowhere in sight,

I know I had closed the gate, locked it tight.

I ran to tell Mother, "Our lamb was gone."

Father walked in and said, "What is wrong?"

"Father, the lamb is missing,
he's left his pen!"

Father said, "We must search
for him, so let's begin!"

All morning we searched hard and
long – but our lamb was nowhere –

He was truly gone!

My Father said, "We must have
a lamb for sacrifice today,

I'll buy one at the temple gate;
I must be on my way!"

(Matthew 21:12, Mark 11:15-16,
Luke 19:45-46)

We celebrated Passover that night
once Father was home.

However, I couldn't think of anything
but my lamb being alone.

The night seemed to drag on forever,

the Passover celebration didn't
make me feel better.

(Exodus 12:24-28, Numbers 9:11-12)

Father left early the next morning,

he had rushed out without any warning.

Then before noon, he came home
with my lamb on his shoulder.

He said he had found him caught in
some thorns near a boulder.

(Genesis 22:13)

He also said he had seen a man in the city,

who was beaten, bloody, dirty and gritty.

He was carrying a cross and on his head a crown of thorns,

his clothes were bloody, tattered and torn.

Trying to recall, remember that familiar face,

suddenly Father realized it was Rabbi
Jesus from Lamb selection Day!

(Isaiah 52:14, Matthew 27:27-31)

As soon as Father finished
speaking, the sky grew
darker than night,

we all thought we had
surely lost our sight.

Then the earth began to
rumble and slowly to shake,

it threw me to the ground.
Mother screamed, "Earthquake!"

When the ground finally
stopped shaking us apart,

the sky grew lighter and
it was no longer dark.

(Matthew 27:45-54)

Father quickly ran to the temple, to kneel and to pray,

he wanted to understand the strange happenings of that day.

But as he approached the temple door,

he saw the priests all in an uproar.

They were wringing their hands and pulling their robes,

"Nothing like this has happened before,

the temple veil is torn. How can we sacrifice today?

Take your offerings, all be on your way!"

"The curtain is torn from the top to the bottom."

It was more than any of them could fathom.

(Matthew 27:51, Mark 15:38-39, Luke 23:44-46)

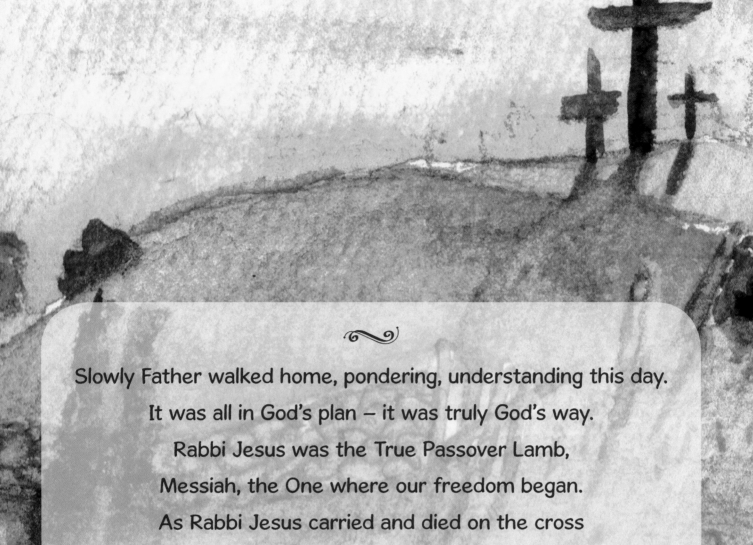

Slowly Father walked home, pondering, understanding this day.

It was all in God's plan – it was truly God's way.

Rabbi Jesus was the True Passover Lamb,

Messiah, the One where our freedom began.

As Rabbi Jesus carried and died on the cross

he realized His blood was the payment, our cost.

Jesus' shed blood was our heavenly gain,

the final Lamb of God would majestically reign!

Father said since this Jesus Messiah was the True Passover Lamb,

as a family, we would never sacrifice another one again!

He said my little lamb was ours to keep – perfect and spot-free!

This Last Lamb – Jesus Messiah – had already
sacrificed himself for my family and me.

**(John 1:29, 36-37, I Corinthians 5:7, 1
Peter1:18-21, Revelations 5:6-14)**

Little did we know more amazing
happenings were on the way,

three days following that crucifixion day!

**(Matthew 17:23, Matthew 27:63, Matthew 28:5-7,
Luke 9:22, Luke 24: 6-8, Luke 24:13-27)**

CPSIA information can be obtained
at www.ICGtesting.com
Printed in the USA
LVIC042037240212
270353LV00005B